ABRAHAM

Destination By Faith

CONNIE SHAIN

WestBow
PRESS
A DIVISION OF THOMAS NELSON
& ZONDERVAN

Unless otherwise noted, all Scripture quotations are taken from the New King James Version
(NKJV), Copyright 1982 by Thomas Nelson, Inc. Used by permission. All rights reserved.

Scripture quotations marked (ESV) are taken from The Holy Bible, English Standard Version. Copyright
2000, 2001 by Crossway Bibles, a division of Good News Publishers. Used by permission. All rights reserved.

Scripture quotations marked (KJV) are from the King James Version of the Bible (public domain).

Scripture quotations marked (NIV) are from the Holy Bible, New International Version,
copyright 1973, 1978, 1984, 2011 by Biblica, Inc. Used by permission. All rights reserved.

Cover photo by author's grandson, Triston Wilkinson

WestBow Press books may be ordered through booksellers or by contacting:

WestBow Press
A Division of Thomas Nelson & Zondervan
1663 Liberty Drive
Bloomington, IN 47403
www.westbowpress.com
1 (866) 928-1240

Because of the dynamic nature of the Internet, any web addresses or links contained in
this book may have changed since publication and may no longer be valid. The views
expressed in this work are solely those of the author and do not necessarily reflect the views
of the publisher, and the publisher hereby disclaims any responsibility for them.

Any people depicted in stock imagery provided by Thinkstock are models,
and such images are being used for illustrative purposes only.
Certain stock imagery © Thinkstock.

ISBN: 978-1-4908-9278-8 (sc)
ISBN: 978-1-4908-9279-5 (e)

Library of Congress Control Number: 2015913944

Print information available on the last page.

WestBow Press rev. date: 11/11/2015

CONTENTS

INTRODUCTION

Some may say that no man's life has been more profoundly influential to generations to come than that of Abraham. Apart from the Lord Jesus Christ, this man's presence on earth may have had farther-reaching impact than any other man throughout the course of time.

One might wonder how one common person like you or me could be used by God in such an uncommon way. How could that human be allowed to hear the voice of God in such a manner that in the end no person or purpose was allowed to speak louder?

Abram—whose name God later changed to Abraham—was a descendant of Seth, the son of humanity's first man and woman, Adam and Eve. God set Abraham apart for Himself to become the nation of Israel. From this nation would emerge the promised Messiah, Jesus Christ. He heard and heeded the voice of God in such a way that the future for mankind became one of hope and redemption instead of hopelessness and despair.

Those alive during the time of Abraham likely would not have known the significant role that this man was to play in God's redemptive plan for all mankind. Could anyone have known that salvation for sinful man would rest not upon the forthcoming Old Testament Law but upon the fulfillment of that Law, Abraham's seed Jesus Christ? Surely Abraham himself did not immediately understand his part in the marvelous story of God's great reclamation. And he could not have known how his faith in Almighty God would largely determine the very destiny of his own life.

As we journey together through this four-week study, my prayer for you will be that God Himself will grant you a new and greater understanding of God's wonderful story of redemption. And through this revelation may you begin to recognize the important part that the Old Testament patriarch Abraham played in that amazing story.

His biblical story begins as God commanded Abraham to leave his ancestral home and to travel and possess the land of Canaan. But even upon his arrival at the Promised Land, opposition awaited. We will witness, as we follow the journey of Abraham's life, that while he became the father of this great nation, his life, though divinely chosen, was really no different than yours and mine. Like so many others it was filled with certain strife and trials as well as normal everyday struggles. Family feuds, marital issues, and even financial woes are certainly nothing new to our generation, and we will read of these very types of incidents playing out in the life of Abraham.

Much of his story includes his experiences in regard to relationships—with a wife, a nephew, his wife's maid, two sons, several kings, and primarily Almighty God Himself. Could God have not accomplished the purpose of redeeming man another way? Could He not have bypassed all the years of Abraham's complicated life and further years to come in the nation of Israel, His chosen people? Of course He could have. But He did not. Instead God chose to use the hardships and difficulties of ordinary people over a period of centuries to bring about His perfect plan of salvation. Abraham—an average man, a man of faith—was one such that God used.

WEEK 1

Promises to Inheritance

Now the LORD had said to Abram:
"Get out of your country,
From your family
And from your father's house,
To a land that I will show you.
I will make you a great nation;
I will bless you
And make your name great;
And you shall be a blessing.
I will bless those who bless you,
And I will curse him who curses you;
And in you all the families of the earth shall be blessed."
(Genesis 12:1–3)

DAY 1

The LORD is trustworthy in all he promises
and faithful in all he does.
—Psalm 145:13, NIV

My hope as you endeavor to journey through this in-depth study is that each day God will uncover and reveal new treasures of truth to you. It is very rewarding before one opens the Word of God to call upon God. For each day's study I am including a small section for you to write a short prayer to God before beginning your study. Just a short one- or two-sentence request from a humble heart is powerful, and you will be amazed by the faithfulness of God as His Word becomes genuinely real and alive to you.

Prayer First: _____

_____

T he definition of the word *promise* is that someone commits herself or himself to ensuring that something will or will not be done. In this first week of our study we will have the privilege of taking a look at the promises that were made by God to His servant Abraham. Surely there is no greater promise keeper than our heavenly Father. A word spoken by almighty God most certainly will come to pass. Hearing the voice of God and remembering that, unlike people, He will not break a promise are both crucial in our walk with God, just as for Abraham. What great assurance it is to know that we can totally trust in the One who by His grace has chosen to make Himself known to Abraham and to us.

It can be said that all seasons of a person's life make up a part of who that individual becomes. God can use all personal relationships, circumstances, and influences as appointments of His providential care. It is no coincidence that God allowed the ancestry of Abraham to be recorded in His Word. Let's begin this study by looking back to Abraham's roots and also get a glimpse of his life at the time that God called him.

Let's begin by reading Genesis 11:10–32.

> Verses 10–26 are an account of the ancestry of Abraham. Starting in verse 27, draw a family tree that begins with Terah. (Those of you adept in genealogy may enjoy going back further than verse 27.) Remember to include branches for the future offspring of Abraham that you can add as our study progresses.

> From verses 27–32, list all the information you can gather about Abraham, his family, and the land they dwelled in.

While we know that Abraham was a descendant of Seth, the text actually begins with the lineage of Shem. It is most interesting to note how God leaves no stones unturned in disclosing to us the history of Abraham and his family. We are given a brief but somewhat descriptive account of those individuals and places that influenced his life from the past and current time as well. The journey of Abraham truly began during those years, but we will take up the journey as we open Genesis 12.

Read Genesis 12:1–3 and Hebrews 11:8.

Many describe this Genesis passage as God's call on Abraham's life.

From verses 1–3, list all that is mentioned that Abraham is required to do. Also list all that is mentioned that God has stated that He will do for Abraham.

From the information we are given in these passages, what specific places does God call Abraham from and to?

Can you recall and record here a time in your life when you knew God was calling you to an act of obedience that required you to go to an unknown place or through uncertain circumstances?

As we walk the journey of life, we, like Abraham, could be required by God to leave our comfort zone and follow God to destinations unknown. It is at these moments that our faith in the Lord can truly be tested the most. Many times the greater the step of faith in God that is required, the greater the purpose and plan that God has in mind. Are you very comfortable in the season or place in life where you are in now? Could God possibly be stirring your heart to move onto a path that has many unanswered questions? Do numerous fears seem to continually enter your mind about what lies ahead?

Abraham was required to do one thing, and that was to leave his homeland. God would do the rest. Our God does not change: as He was with Abraham, He also will be with you. Just remember to act on the last directive He has instructed you to do. He will take care of the rest. And like Abraham, the rest might surely be greater than you ever could have imagined!

You may say that God's voice was unmistakable for Abraham. But what about my life? How can I be certain God has spoken to me? What you sense God is calling you to do may be huge, and certainly you do not want any error in your understanding of God's calling. I would like to share with you four ways in which I believe that God speaks and reveals His will to a believer.

HIS HOLY WORD

Psalm 119:105 (KJV) states, "Thy word is a lamp unto my feet, and a light unto my path." We can be certain that God speaks to us through the reading of His Word. Regular reading, memorization, and meditation upon it will clearly instruct believers in the way that they should go. One can always be sure that the will of God will never contradict His Word. If you are considering a path or an action that is clearly inconsistent with the teaching of His Word, you can be sure that is not the will of God for your life.

GODLY COUNSEL

Proverbs 20:18 (ESV) states, "Plans are established by counsel." Seeking after God's will through the advice of godly counsel is another avenue through which God reveals His will and speaks to a believer. It is very important to always remember to seek advice from a believer that you know walks closely with God and whose life bears evidence of that. Be very leery of secular and unbelieving sources, however wise they may appear to be.

THE HOLY SPIRIT

John 16:13 states, "However, when He, the Spirit of truth, has come, He will guide you into all truth." The Greek word for "guide" in this passage is *hodegeo*, which literally means "to show the way." What assurance we can have knowing that the Holy Spirit will show us the way to go. Keep in mind that while God created us with emotions, they should never be mistaken for the Spirit of God within us.

CIRCUMSTANCES

Proverbs 16:9 states, "A man's heart plans his way, but the Lord directs his steps." It is always important to be discerning of the circumstances that surround you. Often God will engineer the affairs of our lives in such a way that doors will be open and opportunities will arise that lay the course we are to choose. Be careful of pushing doors open and also ignoring happenings that are possibly God's plans presenting themselves.

Spending time in prayer and listening to God are always needed if you believe God has spoken to you and is directing you to a course of action you should take. It is key to remember that Abraham was surely in the position to hear God speak. As was stated earlier, the voice that he heard was unmistakably God's. It was an all-powerful voice that would allow no other to drown it out!

DAY 2

For with God nothing will be impossible.
—LUKE 1:37

Prayer First: _____

_____

O ne can only begin to imagine the many thoughts that were going through the mind of Abraham. A huge revelation had been given to him. The fulfillment of great promises was in store, but also great faith in God would be needed. It is also interesting to consider and wonder about the conversations that occurred between Abraham and Sarah and speculate as to whether Sarah was quickly willing to obey her husband and the Lord and leave her home as well. My personal opinion is that because God chose to include her in His great Hall of Faith in Hebrews 11, regardless of her fears and feelings, she willingly stepped out in faith in what clearly seemed to be an impossible set of circumstances to overcome. Today's study should give us a little more understanding as to why the situation seemed impossible.

Picking back up in our study, let's read Genesis 12:1–3 again along with Genesis 13:14–16.

What do you find about these verses that might be puzzling, in view of what is spoken about Abraham's wife Sarah in chapter 11?

We previously read in Genesis 11 that Abraham's wife Sarah was barren and had no children. Abraham must have questioned in his mind how a childless man could produce a great nation. To uproot one's family in the midst of a seemingly impossible situation surely to Abraham was a challenging test. But we read that God promised to Abraham that his descendants would become as plentiful as the dust of the earth. Can dust be counted? It is obvious that the number is too vast to tell. With certainty the impossible situation became possible by the hand of the One controlling the situation: almighty God! In my own life I have often found myself focusing on the hard or even seemingly impossible aspects of a current dilemma. But then I would receive a quick reminder from God's Holy Spirit that the God of my impossible situation was the same God of Abraham's. *Those reminders usually manage to bring my thoughts and perspective in line with God's truth.*

Genesis 12:2 states that God will bless Abraham and make his name great.

In your own words record what you believe God was communicating to Abraham in this statement.

Do you believe that Abraham completely understood these words spoken by God?

The Hebrew word for "bless" in this passage is *barak*, pronounced "baw-rak," which means "to bless God as act of adoration or vice versa, man as a benefit." Surely such an honor for God to bestow upon a man would cause his name to be remembered for generations to come. The phrase "you shall be a blessing" also implies a divine command by God that we shall later see fulfilled in Abraham's life. We will learn that Abraham became a man of great wealth and influence. But the full implications of this promise at the time may or may not have been known by Abraham. Undoubtedly the fact that the Lord had spoken to Abraham must have revealed to him that something beyond ordinary could be in store.

Let's look a little closer at Genesis 12:3.

Do you conclude that God was only referring to Abraham as the object of His blessing when He spoke verse 3a, or could this blessing include others?

In regard to this short passage, what observations might be made concerning the United States and its relationship with modern-day Israel?

The same Hebrew word that is used for bless in verse 2a, *barak*, is also used in verse 3. The Hebrew word for curse in this passage is *arar*, pronounced "aw-rar," which is translated "execrate," the definition being "to hate." What a scary thought to be on the receiving end and be the object of almighty God's hatred. This significant promise that God made was directed to all those who blessed and all who cursed Abraham and his descendants. While God is certainly not obligated to give a reason for blessing certain nations as He does, many might say that one reason the United States has been on the receiving end of such an outpouring of blessing is because of their ongoing friendly relationship with the nation of Israel.

Read Genesis 18:18; 22:18; 26:4b; 28:14b; Matthew 1:1; Acts 3:25–26.

From Genesis 12:3b and considering all these passages, how through Abraham would all families of the earth be blessed?

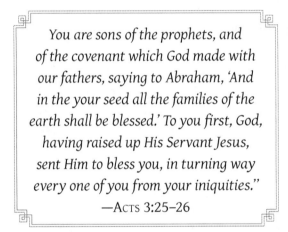

You are sons of the prophets, and of the covenant which God made with our fathers, saying to Abraham, 'And in the your seed all the families of the earth shall be blessed.' To you first, God, having raised up His Servant Jesus, sent Him to bless you, in turning way every one of you from your iniquities."
—Acts 3:25–26

This final and most telling promise was that all families on earth would be blessed through the Jewish people. God fulfilled this promise through Abraham's "seed," Jesus Christ. God had already set in motion a plan whereby He set apart a people that were called His own. In that plan the promised Messiah would come from those chosen people. God always has a purpose for all that He does even if that purpose is not accomplished till several generations later. How exciting to see the story of redemption beginning to unfold even as early as these Old Testament times!

DAY 3

Then the LORD appeared to Abram and said, "To your descendants I will give this land." And there he built an altar to the LORD, who had appeared to him.
—Genesis 12:7

Prayer First: _____

_____

When pondering on the thoughts of all the circumstances that surrounded Abraham and Sarah's journey and arrival in Canaan, it is probably safe to assume that they experienced the normal struggles that any family moving today might experience. They just did not know the luxury of a moving van pulling up into their drive and loading up their possessions. For the one who has experienced the life-changing event of a move, today's study might shed new light on the faithfulness of God shown to Abraham.

Read Genesis 12:4–9; 13:14–18.

In verses 4–6 we learn the details of Abraham's journey and arrival in Canaan. What important fact about the land do we find revealed in 12:6?

When God called Abraham, He pronounced to him that He would take him to a land that He would later reveal. In these passages we find that promise fulfilled as God appeared to Abraham and introduced him to what would subsequently become the land of Israel. In chapter 13 God revealed to Abraham that the land he and his many descendants would receive would extend as far as the eyes could see. We also find that the land was occupied by the Canaanites, which obviously could have been a bit of an obstacle. These people were always considered the enemy of Israel. These encounters with God, in the midst of what Abraham knew could be fierce opposition to come, surely were timely to say the least. Let's examine a little more in depth these two meetings and their spiritual application to our current lives.

Read again Genesis 12:7; 13:14–18.

> In each of these instances God again spoke to Abraham. In both occasions what was Abraham's response to God as a result of these encounters?

> Can you recall and record here a significant time in your life when God spoke to you (maybe not with an audible voice), making known to you the realization of His presence? Record any remembrance of where you were and what your response to the encounter was.

With certainty most of us can look back upon our lives and recognize those instances where God's Holy Spirit impressed upon us so vividly that without a doubt we knew that our Maker had spoken. In looking back, it is interesting to note that almost always we can remember exactly where we were at the time. For me these usually have occurred during a time of trial or struggle and were exactly what I needed at the time. When these encounters occurred in Abraham's life, his first response was to build an altar. Surely for Abraham as well as for us this place of remembrance is where God has inspired us to continue trusting Him as we walk the road of life. We like Abraham face many uncertainties. When God favors us with these divine appointments, it is for our encouragement, but also it is for His greater purpose. In the midst of these manifestations, if we recognize the presence of God and take heed, we too will be like Abraham and become a blessing to many.

DAY 4

*Now there was a famine in the land, and Abram went down to Egypt
to dwell there, for the famine was severe in the land.*
—Genesis 12:10

Prayer First: _____

_____

Abraham and Sarah had made it through uprooting their lives and arrived at the Promised Land. One might think that surely, after such a huge step of faith, God would not have allowed another test in their lives. But it seems that one is on the horizon. Most of us can relate that sometimes tests in our lives can come in twos and maybe more. We are not exempt from struggles that God may allow, however many or difficult they may be. In today's lesson let's take a look at Abraham's and Sarah's response to a hardship that had come upon them.

Read Genesis 12:10–20.

Explain in detail the reason for Abraham and Sarah leaving Canaan and all the happenings that occurred during their stay in Egypt.

Do you believe that this journey to Egypt was God's perfect will for Abraham and Sarah? Why or why not?

Can you describe an "Egypt" in your life that you went to in response to a famine-like situation? (This does not necessarily mean just lacking physical means. It could be other types of struggles such as an emotional or spiritual situation.)

How often have many of us like Abraham found ourselves in very difficult situations because of decisions we have made? When the droughts in our lives occur, we sometimes end up in "Egypt" before we realize it. We can easily get caught up in a web of deceit just as Abraham did. He was fearful for his life, and in all reality Sarah was his half-sister. But even though it might have appeared to be justified, half-truth is still untruth.

Just a little heads-up. Be on the lookout. We might see this scene played out similarly in Abraham's life again. But what we will also recognize is God's miraculous protection and grace upon Abraham's and Sarah's life. God had a plan, and it would not be hindered. He also has a plan for your life that will not be prevented from occurring. If you find yourself in a "drought" in life or even have gone so far as entering "Egypt," you can call upon the merciful, gracious God of Abraham, and He will be there for you.

DAY 5

Arise, walk in the land through its length and its width, for I give it to you.
—Genesis 13:17

Prayer First: _____

_____

Many may wonder if the destination that God had for Abraham included Egypt along the way. While we may not know for certain, we do know that Canaan was the inheritance that God had chosen to give to him. Thankfully in today's lesson we find that Abraham and Sarah make their way back to that land.

Read Genesis 13

In this passage we see that Abraham went back to the land that God had originally commanded him to enter. In order for there to be no strife between Abraham and Lot and their herdsmen, what agreement did they arrange?

On what basis did Lot make his decision when choosing which land he would inhabit?

If you have previously studied this story, consider what you know of the future that was in store for Lot and Abraham. List what guiding principles you can learn by observing these men's examples of decision making and how these principles could apply to your life today as well.

(If you are not familiar with the life of Abraham it is ok to leave this question unanswered. It is possible that you might want to come back to it at a later date, but some information on Abraham's future is actually given in this passage.)

I find it very interesting that as Abraham returned to Canaan, we are told, he was a very wealthy man. He surely could have chosen to dwell anywhere he desired, but because he desired peace in his family, he allowed Lot to make the decision. Because of the previous drought it is possible that Lot made that decision based on the fact that the land was well watered. It might have appeared like the Garden of Eden. But the passage states that the people in Sodom were exceedingly wicked. It is very important to remember that a lush outward appearance does not always indicate that all is well. Sometimes the consequences of our decisions are not immediate. But as time progresses, those ramifications will eventually become evident. It is interesting to observe that while Abraham was humble and desired no strife, God's providential hand was all along protecting him. But the same cannot be said for Lot. He was headed for a future disastrous place and was utterly unaware of it. We will soon learn more about Lot and his life after he made his dwelling in Sodom.

WEEK 2

Rescue to Covenant

And he believed in the LORD, and He counted it to him for righteousness.
—GENESIS 15:6

DAY 1

They also took Lot, Abram's brother's son who dwelt in Sodom, and his goods and departed.
—Genesis 14:12

Prayer First: _____

_____

Hats off to you! You have already finished a week of our study. How thankful I am to God that He has preserved His Word and we are allowed to take this journey together. Already we are beginning to learn how crucially important it is to recognize and heed the voice of God. While surely we cannot hinder the providential plan of God, we certainly can make life difficult for ourselves and those around us when we fail in these two areas.

I hope you are rested up and ready to go because Week 2 is jam-packed full. Genesis 14 and 15 bring to light great, marvelous truths, there to be uncovered like nuggets of gold. I will not expound any more but will let you explore and discover these truths yourself as we open up His Word together again.

Read Genesis 14:1–12.

From these verses make a list of kings and their land who fought against one another.

(Four against five).

Also describe what occurred in this battle of the Valley of Siddim.

Who is a familiar name in this passage, and what happens to him?

Lot's life may be considered an illustration of what can happen to one who seeks after earthly means and not the will of God. In many instances, enslavement or bondage occurs when people choose what looks attractive or what might bring temporary or momentary satisfaction. Satan, our enemy, knows precisely how to set us up before striking and applying the chains. An example of this in a more personally applicable way could be the many types of addictions that numerous people are controlled by.

In studying this passage and reading about the battle of the Valley of Siddim, I found myself read and rereading it just to try to understand and comprehend all that was occurring. Even over time many aspects of life never seem to change. People somehow manage to continue waging war against one another as evil runs rampant among a nation. Surely during Abraham's journey, while God was bringing about the plan for the Messiah, He was also revealing the need for the Messiah.

Now read Genesis 14:13–16.

From these few verses, what can we learn about the individual who reported to Abraham that Lot had been captured and about those who surrounded Abraham in the place where he dwelled?

What immediately did Abraham do when he heard the news of Lot? Also describe his pursuit and the strategy he used.

Consider now a loved one who spiritually or physically could be in bondage to the enemy. To what lengths will you go to rescue that loved one from the enemy? What strategy will you use?

Take this time to record what the enemy may have stolen from you and how you have taken it back or plan to recover it in the future. (This may be a very private answer that you prefer not to share with others).

We do not know exactly how much time had passed since Lot had entered Sodom when he was taken captive. We do know that it seems just one short chapter ago it appeared to Lot that Sodom was the place to be. Obviously now we are beginning to recognize the consequences that came to Lot as a result of the choice he made. Ironically at the time when Abraham accepted the remaining land, it did not appear to be the prime property. But all along this was God's choice place for him to be. He surely was a wealthy man and was surrounded by many who were his allies. When hearing of the attack and Lot's captivity, he wasted no time in pursuing the enemy and taking back his nephew and also everything the enemy had stolen. Like Abraham, we can pursue the enemy and take back everything that has been stolen from us.

DAY 2

Prayer First: _____

_____

Our lesson today may be a bit short in length but not in meaning. In our text we will find that Abraham was greeted by the King of Sodom and the King of Salem but interestingly enough it almost appears that he ignored Sodom's king until after he celebrated in worship with Melchizedek, the priest of God Most High.

Read Genesis 14:17–24; Psalm 110; Hebrews 7.

Describe from these verses all you learn about Melchizedek and any new insight that God reveals to you about this priest of the Most High God?

The appearance of this King of Salem can bring to one's mind many questions. Who was this priest of "God Most High"? Where did he come from?

In the beginning of our study you drew a family tree from information that was gathered from the Scripture in regard to God's servant Abraham. But no place in God's Word do we find any record of the lineage of Melchizedek. No information is divulged about his beginning or his end. A very peculiar person indeed. But a little more research of the Scriptures shows that in the book of Hebrews the writer compares this priest to another High Priest, the Lord Jesus Christ. I find it very interesting that we do not know for certain the human author of the book of Hebrews. That and the appearance of this mystery man can leave one with many questions remaining unanswered.

What we can take away from this passage is that Melchizedek blessed Abraham. Abraham then recognized him as a true priest of the living God and in return gave him a tithe of all. This is the first mention of tithing in the Bible. Surely as God blesses us, we too will want to give back to our God a tithe of all that we have received.

DAY 3

Behold the proud, His soul is not upright in him; But the just shall live by his faith.
—Habakkuk 2:4

Prayer First: _____

_____

It seems the farther we move along in the life of Abraham, the more exciting it gets. In today's study we will find that God blesses him with another encounter with Himself. But even more thrilling is the very first introduction in God's Word of faith and righteousness associated together.

Read Genesis 15:1-6.

What occurred to Abraham again in Genesis 15:1? Record God's first words to him.

Read Matthew 14:22–27; Revelation 1:12–18.

From each of these verses, what occurred that caused each person to be afraid?

What was the Lord's response to each?

Time and again throughout Scripture, we find that when individuals have encounters with the holy God, the first words He communicates to them are "Do not be afraid." Some sources have stated that the phrase "fear not" is used 272 times in the Old and New Testaments. Another source states 365 times. While I'm not exactly sure of the number, I am exactly sure that either number is enough for me. Obviously a reverential fear of God comes upon those who come into His presence. God's continual reassuring words of "fear not" throughout the Scripture are a certain indicator that peace is what He desires for us. Jesus' very words when He appeared to the disciples after the resurrection were "Peace be with you."

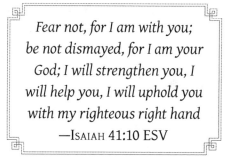

Fear not, for I am with you; be not dismayed, for I am your God; I will strengthen you, I will help you, I will uphold you with my righteous right hand
—Isaiah 41:10 ESV

When God chose again to reveal Himself to Abraham, He told him not to be afraid. He also stated that He would protect him and be his reward. For God to declare that He Himself was an exceedingly great reward surely attests that a relationship with the Almighty is better than any earthly crown.

History reveals that according to the customs in this time period a man without natural heirs would adopt a child to be his foremost heir. This person could even be a slave. If later the man had a biological child that child would replace the adopted one as the leading heir.

Abraham must have believed that through an adopted heir God would bring him many descendants. However, God made it clear that his descendants would come through his own flesh and blood and would be as many as the stars in the sky. Abraham's response to this revelation in Genesis 15:6 truly reveals one of the most profound truths found in Scripture.

> From Genesis 15:6 what was Abraham's response to the message God had declared to him?

Surely Abraham didn't try to analyze it or figure it all out. He merely believed that God would do what He said He would do. At that point he chose to believe God no matter how impossible the situation seemed.

Who could imagine that merely believing God would qualify one for righteousness? Wouldn't it have taken spotless living and pure devotion to Almighty God? But how was one to become pure in God's eyes? Ironically the story of Abraham is all a part of God's plan of how one could become pure in God's eyes. Only by the shed blood of Jesus Christ can that purity occur—Jesus Christ, the "seed" of Abraham whom through all the earth would be blessed.

Let's take a look at a few other passages that state what in God's eyes declares us righteous.

Read Habakkuk 2:2–4; Romans 1:17; Romans 4; Galatians 3:1–14.

> From these passages list all the things you learn about being justified by God through faith.

If God declares us just for living our lives by faith what schemes might Satan, the enemy, use to try to deceive us and cause us to stumble?

List opportunities in your life you have to walk by faith instead of by sight.

Wow, what a strong statement was made in Scripture when Abraham's belief in God (notice it wasn't his works) was counted as righteousness! That really just goes against the grain of our thinking. How different our lives would be if we just could grasp that one principle.

So often we are not going to know what happens next. We want to have everything figured out before proceeding, but if we did, would we really need God? Of course not! Salvation and living the Christian life are through faith in God from first to last. Looking back from the moment the Lord called Abraham to leave his home until now in Genesis 15, all that Abraham was really required to do was to believe God. Most likely he and Sarah ended up in a mess in Egypt because he did not do that very thing. One might ask wasn't he required to obey? Most assuredly he was. Belief and obedience go hand in hand. In all actuality disobedience to God is merely another form of unbelief in God.

I can truly testify to the fact that when God revealed to me through Scripture that righteousness in God's eyes was based not upon works but upon faith my life was changed. That freedom caused me to want to obey God!

DAY 4

Then He said to him, "I am the LORD, who brought you out of Ur of the Chaldeans, to give you this land to inherit it."
—Genesis 15:7

Prayer First: _____

_____

Yesterday's study was rich in the principles taught in God's Word regarding faith and righteousness. How could God follow that? But today we will find that He most certainly can and does. Take a look as we dissect the next verse, Genesis 15:7.

Now look at Genesis 15:7–8.

What three important points did God remind Abraham of in verse 7?

Now take some time to reflect on your life. For some this may require looking back at some painful moments or even painful seasons that you have experienced. But it can be very rewarding and reveal the praise worthiness of our God. (These recordings can be private between you and the Lord if you choose.)

1. List all that God has spoken to you (through His Word, prayer, etc.) in regard to who He is to you personally.

2. List from your life where God has brought you from and all that He has brought you out of.

3. List all that God has revealed to you (through His Word, prayer, etc.) that He has planned for your future.

One can conclude that packed into verse 7 are three huge statements made by God. God chose in this verse to remind Abraham of who He was, what He had done for Abraham, and what He intended to do for him. One should probably sit and meditate on this one verse for quite some time. Recording what God has shown you as to who He is, what He has brought you out of, and what He has planned for you most likely is a very lengthy list. By all means reflecting on this list should definitely increase one's faith in Almighty God as it did Abraham's. Obviously Abraham was requesting a sign of the promise that God had made and was not speaking in unbelief in verse 8. In the remainder of chapter 15 we will study God's answer to that request.

DAY 5

And it came to pass, when the sun went down and it was dark, that behold, there appeared a smoking oven and a burning torch that passed between those pieces.
—Genesis 15:17

Prayer First: _____

_____

If anyone has ever stated that the Bible is unexciting and uninteresting, he or she has not read Genesis 15. The story in today's lesson is captivating and fascinating to say the least. I would suggest that you say an extra prayer to God, asking Him to reveal a glimpse of His Holiness displayed in this amazing passage.

Read again Genesis 15:9–21.

List from verses 9–11 all that the Lord instructs Abraham to do and Abraham's actions to follow.

Describe what occurred in verse 12.

Read Exodus 1 and Exodus 12:40–42.

Do you find any connection between the Exodus passages and Genesis 15:12–16? If so, record your findings here.

Now let's take a moment to step back in Genesis to the second chapter. There we will find another instance where the presence of God came upon a man in a somewhat similar way.

Read Genesis 2:21–23.

In reading Genesis 2:21–23, we learn of another occasion when God caused an individual to fall into a deep sleep. Give some thought to the creation of humanity and the fall into sin. What was the principal difference between Adam's life and Abraham's life during these deep sleeps?

The Hebrew word *tardemah* used for deep sleep is the same word used for Adam's sleep in Genesis 2. When God allowed this trance to fall upon Adam, sin had not entered the human race. Woman was created then, and life and hope was the future for mankind. When God chose to allow a deep sleep to fall upon Abraham, horror and darkness arrived.

It was at this time that He showed him the future of the Israelite people and the oppression and slavery that would come upon them. But also at this time He communicated that He would not leave them in bondage but would rescue them and return them to a place of freedom. The vision of the future for the descendants of Abraham can be described as a picture of humankind in the sinful state—enslavement and captivity to sin from which only God can liberate us. In the book of Exodus we read about the Deliverer that God sent to the Hebrew people, a man named Moses. In the New Testament we can read about our Deliverer, the Lord Jesus Christ!

Look now again at Genesis 15:17–21.

Describe from verse 17 what occurred during Abraham's deep sleep.

List how the Lord is described in each of these passages. While there are many more throughout Scripture we could research, for the sake of time we will limit our search to these few.

Exodus 19:17–18.

Psalm 18:6–8.

Isaiah 6:1–4.

Isaiah 31:9.

Revelation 15:8.

> *Now Mount Sinai*
> *was completely in smoke,*
> *because the LORD descended*
> *upon it in fire. Its smoke*
> *ascended like the smoke of*
> *a furnace, and the whole*
> *mountain quaked greatly.*
> —EXODUS 19:18

Considering how God is represented in these passages, what insight do you gain concerning the smoking oven and the burning torch in verse 17?

Look up the word *covenant* in the dictionary, and if you are familiar with word studies, do one on the Hebrew word for "covenant" as it is used in Genesis 15:18. Record what you learn from your study time.

What important promise did God make to Abraham in this covenant?

Did God place any conditions on the promise to Abraham?

Do you have any insight as to why God listed the nations of the land that he would give to Abraham's descendants?

As we consider the passages listed above we can correctly assume that the Lord is represented throughout the Scriptures by fire and smoke. As well in this instance, the glory of the Lord was shown to Abraham by the smoking oven and burning torch. In these Old Testament times a covenant ceremony was performed where by two individuals passed between bloody pieces of slaughtered animals and birds. These individuals were considered to be equal parties in terms of relationship. But the Lord and Abraham were not equal parties. In this covenant only the Lord passed through the sacrificial animals. This arrangement represented Holy God stooping down to sinful humanity as a gift of grace. It is very important to remember that this was an unconditional covenant made by God with Abraham. Terms were not set by any conditions placed upon Abraham's actions.

On this day we see that God promises to the descendants of Abraham the land of Canaan, which would later become the land of Israel. He defined the boundaries by naming the rivers and listed the nations to be taken over by the Israelites. On the same day that Abraham believed God and was counted as righteous, the Lord established the Abrahamic covenant. Could there be any connection?

WEEK 3

Ishmael to Intercession

When Abram was ninety-nine years old, the LORD appeared to Abram and said to him, "I am Almighty God; walk before Me and be blameless. And I will make My covenant between Me and you, and will multiply you exceedingly."
—Genesis 17:1–2

DAY 1

He shall be a wild man; His hand shall be against every man,
And every man's hand against him.
And he shall dwell in the presence of all his brethren.
—Genesis 16:12

Prayer First: _____

_____

It's hard to believe we are halfway through our study. I can hardly wait to travel on as we begin week 3. The glory of the Lord represented through fire and smoke does not seem to just smolder in my mind but continues to burn in the form of a huge flame. Surely that flame will burn higher and brighter as we continue to add spiritual chunks of God's Word.

Let us briefly now look at the story of Hagar and Ishmael. We will not spend a lot of study time here, but it is important to have knowledge of the relationship between Ishmael and the promised son, Isaac, in order to better understand God's redemptive plan for mankind through the life of his servant Abraham. In another display of God's grace, begin to watch the exciting changes that occur in Abraham's and Sarah's life in spite of their own strategy to try to fulfill that plan.

Read Genesis 16

List the ways that Sarah and Abraham tried to fulfill God's plan by forming their own plan.

While the ten commandments had not been given yet, in what ways did their plan go against what we know now to be God's basic ordinances for people?

Can you think of a time in your life when you stepped ahead of God and devised your own plan concerning the state of affairs of your life? If you answered yes, what were the consequences of those actions?

So often many of us, like Sarah and Abraham lack faith in God at certain times and possibly think He needs our help along the way. While God is merciful and gracious to us, there are still consequences as a result of our taking matters into our own hands.

These consequences are far-reaching and sometimes affect the lives of many people. The phrase "His hand shall be against every man" spoken by the Angel of the Lord does bear much significance. The "Wild Man," Ishmael, and his descendants will ever be at war with their brethren. It certainly does shed some light upon the current state of the Middle East. The Arabs who are descendants of Ishmael and the Israelites who are descendants of Isaac are the remaining people, while the nations of Genesis 15:19–21 no longer exist.

The "Angel of the Lord" that appeared to Hagar in this passage is believed to be a theophany or specifically a Christophany, an appearance of the preincarnate Christ. The fact that God communicated with Hagar demonstrates His great kindness and justice to all mankind.

DAY 2

No longer shall your name be called Abram, but your name shall be Abraham; for I have made you a father of many nations.
—GENESIS 17:5

Prayer First: _____

_____

Most of us don't spend a lot of time thinking about names, specifically the names of people or their meanings. But today's lesson might be considered a crash course on that very subject. Let's take a look at God's name that is used in this particular passage. Also changes are coming for Abraham and Sarah. Does that possibly mean that changes could come for you and me as well? Well, maybe not on this earth but quite certainly we can plan on it in eternity!

Read Genesis 17

In verse 1 God again appears to Abraham. Who does He identify Himself as? List any insight that you may have received about the true nature and meaning of this name.

What if any differences do you find concerning the way that God appears to Abraham in this passage in comparison to His appearance to Abraham in Genesis 15?

In this passage we find that the Lord appears to Abraham for the fourth time after he enters the land of Canaan. But for the first time He reveals Himself as El Shad-dah'ee, "The Almighty." The word can be described in that it can be much the same as a mountain. God's strength and endurance can be compared to a mountain that with all certainty is huge. That endurance surely reveals to us the faithfulness of God. Obviously a mountain does not go away.

Also it is interesting to observe that God's appearance to Abraham in this chapter was not in a vision as it was in chapter 15. It is probable that according to God's design, after He called Abraham in Genesis 12, He later gave Abraham a vision in chapter 15 of what the future would hold. Chapter 17 is God in His perfect timing shedding light upon Abraham's journey, and had Abraham waited on that light in chapter 16, much difficulty could have been avoided. So often many of us are given a vision of what God has willed for us to do but jump ahead in the darkness and do not wait for God's light to shine upon our path. Thankfully, that light still does shine, and regardless of our actions that were taken in the darkness, God's plan still prevails!

Also in verse 1 of Genesis 17 God instructs Abraham to walk before Him and be perfect. List any new understanding you have acquired about the word "perfect" or "blameless" as used in some translations.

As we learned earlier, God's acceptance of Abraham was based not on his works but on the faith that he exhibited. But He does demand purity of those He uses in notable ways. The Hebrew word for perfect comes from *tamiym*, pronounced "taw-meem," meaning "entire"; another meaning is "integrity." God was commanding Abraham to live a life that adhered to moral and ethical principles. This also implied a duty to walk before Him honestly and have a soundness of character. God will not allow dishonesty and corruption to be present in the lives of His servants.

God again tells Abraham in this passage that He will multiply his descendants. What significant change occurs in verse 5, and why?

At this point let's move ahead a few verses. What also occurs to Sarah in verses 15–16?

The name Abram means "Exalted Father," and Abraham means "Father of Many." While his principal descendants were the Israelites, he also was the father of Ishmael and the Arab nations and later other offspring from Keturah, a concubine. From this point on he will be referred to as Abraham.

The name Sarai signifies "my Princess"(to one family only). Sarah signifies "a Princess" (namely of multitudes). The new name given represents a new involvement or relationship with God. She was given a divine promise, and the change of her name was a ratification of that promise.

Let us now look at a couple more instances in Scripture where God has changed the name of a person or persons. Write down the former name and the new name and any information you acquire as to why God changed their names. (Example: what He already had in mind for his future; Matthew 16:18.)

Genesis 32:22–32.

John 1:35–42.

Read Revelation 2:17 and Revelation 3:12.

From these passages what names are identified with those who "overcome"?

What significance can be found to you in:

The new name you will be given in eternity?

The names you will be identified with as a pillar in the Temple of God?

It is very obvious from Scripture that the names we are identified with are significant to God. In speaking to the faithful church in Philadelphia the writer John tells in Revelation that he who "overcomes" will be made a pillar in the temple of God. When I think of a pillar, I think of a beautiful white huge building and the pillars are the first things that I see. They are strong and prominent, enduring and steady. While in heaven the temple will not need support to stand, what magnificent reward is given to the faithful one who overcomes. On the pillar will be written "the name of God, the name of the city of God, and the new name of Christ." Obviously we see that much importance is placed by God on a name.

> *Who is he who overcomes the world, but he who believes that Jesus is the Son of God?*
> —1 JOHN 5:5

As I write this my daughter is expecting her third child, my fifth grandchild. The subject of many of our conversations is what will his name be? At this point she and her husband have not come up with just that perfect name. Think that throughout our lives we are so closely identified with our names. It is who we become. In eternity we will become identified with the name of God, the city of God, and the name of Christ. This could be glory beyond description! How gracious and loving of our God to give us just a glimpse of that glory here on earth through this magnificent passage in the book of Revelation!

DAY 3

You have been estranged from Christ, you who attempt to be justified by law; you have fallen from grace. For we through the Spirit eagerly wait for the hope of righteousness by faith.
—GALATIANS 5:4–5

Prayer First: _____

_____

I believe you will find today's study a bit intriguing as you begin to understand the connection of the "Abrahamic covenant" with God's Law and the two sons of Abraham. As we see God's plan of redemption continuing to unfold, it is as if more pieces of the puzzle continue to fall into place.

Now let's take a closer look at the covenant that God made with Abraham. From Genesis 17, list all that you learn about God's covenant with Abraham, including promises that were made by God to Abraham.

In this chapter the act of circumcision of every male child and Abraham himself was the sign of the covenant between God and Abraham. While God promised to bless Ishmael, He revealed that this covenant would be established through Abraham's and Sarah's son Isaac, who would be born one year later. The importance of this command made by God upon Abraham and his descendants is confirmed by verse 14 when God states that those who do not obey this demand have broken His covenant and will be cut off from His people. God again promises to Abraham and his descendants the land of Canaan as an everlasting possession and also promises to be their God.

Let's briefly look at another covenant that God made with His people later in the Old Testament. Skim Exodus 19–23; then read Exodus 24.

List as many details as you can from the Exodus 24 passage about the "old covenant" God made with His people through His servant Moses.

What was the people's responsibility in this covenant?

One can only imagine the sight of such a ceremony as was recorded in Exodus 24! Again we find with this covenant, as with the Abrahamic covenant, a symbolization of Holy God stooping down in grace to sinful man.

> *And Moses took the blood, sprinkled it on the people, and said, "This is the blood of the covenant which the LORD has made with you according to all these words."*
> —Exodus 24:8

Moses declared the words and judgments of the Lord and the people answered in one voice, stating that they would do all that the Lord had said to do. A foreshadowing picture of the sacrifice of the Lord Jesus Christ was the animal sacrifices in these Old Testament times. In this ceremony the sprinkling of the blood on the people was God's actual establishment of His covenant with His people.

It was at this point in the history of man that God made a huge announcement. God's Law was given. Man has been made aware that he does not set the standard for right and acceptable living before a Holy God. God Himself is the one who will set those standards.

As the glory of the Lord rested on Mt. Sinai here again we find the Lord as a consuming fire. Surely that powerful and spectacular presence was breathtaking and humbling to the people. Certainly it inspired them without question to respond in unity with a desire to take heed and obey all the words of the Lord.

But would man in his sinful state be enabled by the Law to keep every word of the Law? Because He could not, the animal sacrifices would continue. Still, as stated earlier, they were only a picture of the ultimate sacrifice to come that would be sufficient to satisfy the requirements of Holy God. That ultimate sacrifice was the Lord Jesus Christ. What was required of man was faith that that very sacrifice was the only satisfactory payment for his sin.

Here again we find that it is faith that is acceptable before God and not works. So why was the Law given? Let's take a look at New Testament passages that will shed some light on this very question.

Read Romans 7:7–25; Galatians 3:15–4:7, 21–31.

From these passages much explanation is given as to why God has given us His Law. Record here what insight you might have received in regard to man's need and God's purpose for the Law.

Since God has given us His Law, are we made children of God by keeping the Law?

If we are required to keep the Law but continually break the Law, what actual state of being are we in?

From reading Galatians 4:1–5 what do we learn that God has done about this enslavement that man finds himself in?

Scripture states that "all have sinned and fall short of the glory of God." Because of this evident truth, all have broken God's Law. Mankind was basically enslaved and in bondage with no hope of ever achieving freedom. This is the story of redemption. "When the fullness of time had come God sent forth His Son, born of a woman, born under the Law, to redeem those who were under the Law ….) In this passage (Galatians 4:4–5), the Greek word translated "redeem" is *exagorazo*, meaning "to buy up, ransom, or figuratively to rescue from loss."

It is only when man recognizes his sinful state that he recognizes his bondage. Many lost individuals are not even aware of their enslavement or their need to be set free. Countless men and women believe that moral and right living is acceptable before God and are unaware that God declares all our righteous acts to be like filthy rags in His sight. They certainly have been taken captive by an enemy and need to be liberated, just as Lot literally needed liberation earlier in our story. All of us have needed deliverance from the yoke of slavery we once found ourselves in. Oh I am so thankful that He has rescued me! How about you?

Read again Galatians 4:21–31 and Romans 9:6–9.

Galatians 4:21–31 talks about the two sons of Abraham and the symbolic meaning associated with their lives. While the promised son Isaac is yet to be born, let's take a look at these passages that clearly distinguish the differences in spiritual application between these two lives.

List all the facts that you can glean from these passages about these two sons.

Isaac

Ishmael

From all that you have gathered how would you compare

The son of the bondwoman (according to the flesh) to the Law?

The son of the freewoman (according to the promise) to faith?

Verse 29 of Galatians 4 states that "as he who was born according to the flesh then persecuted him who was born according to the spirit, even so it is now." Can you relate this in any way to your life presently?

So often we can find ourselves caught in a trap of trying to continually stay "clean" before the Lord. God gave us the Law that we might become aware of our need for redemption. Trying to perfectly follow it sets in motion a pattern of trying to live by the Law but continually breaking the Law, which in turn brings condemnation. This is one of the types of bondage that Satan loves the most. Freedom to live by faith in Jesus, who is the fulfillment of the Law, enables us by His power within us to walk uprightly before the Lord. It is certainly liberating to know that we are children of the freewoman and not of the bondwoman!

DAY 4

For this is the word of promise: "At this time I will come and Sarah shall have a son."
—Romans 9:9

Prayer First: _____

_____

To think that one man could experience so many divine encounters with Holy God! In today's lesson we will learn of another. Just remember in each of these to ask yourself, "What was the reason or purpose for the encounter?" As was stated earlier, it could be for encouragement, but in many instances it could be for instruction or, as in today's lesson, for revelation of future things to come.

Read Genesis 18:1–15.

How did the Lord appear to Abraham in chapter 18:1–2? What could possibly be an explanation for the Lord appearing to Abraham in the form of three men?

It seems that in this encounter with the Lord the focus was on Sarah, where previously it had been upon Abraham. What was the purpose for the Lord's visit with Abraham on this occasion?

In verse 13 the Lord asked why Sarah had laughed when she heard the news that she would bear a child. Why should this cause Sarah to believe that what had been spoken by the Lord was going to occur?

Look up these passages. List what is spoken concerning the thoughts of those mentioned.

Psalm 94:11.

Matthew 9:1–4.

Luke 9:46–48.

As with Sarah and according to the passages you have just studied, what insight is given of God's omniscience, especially in regard to our thoughts?

Read Isaiah 55:8–9.

Let's shift the focus now off our thoughts and place it upon the thoughts of the Almighty. How can this Isaiah passage explain what is taking place in Sarah's life at the time?

> Do these verses in Isaiah give you any comfort or encouragement concerning a trial or a situation you might be walking through at this time in your life?

How encouraging to know that we serve a God who knows our very thoughts. Sometimes I think I know my husband and daughters so well that I know what they are thinking. And they possibly could say that about me as well. But our finite understanding of our loved ones' thinking is based on relationships that develop through time spent with one another. God knows our thoughts because of His unlimited knowledge and understanding of us. He is omniscient. The very fact that He possesses universal and complete knowledge of all things is hard to fathom but can bring great assurance that we are trusting in an all-knowing God. Even though He knew Sarah was thinking that her giving birth to a child in her old age seemed impossible, He knew exactly what was to come and the plan He had in store for Sarah. As was stated in the Isaiah passage, God's thoughts and ways are high above ours.

The Lord's visit to Abraham and Sarah is an example of His complete faithfulness to fulfill the promise He has previously made through the Abrahamic covenant. The visit made by three men could possibly be another "Christophany," one of the men being the Lord and the other two possibly angels. While we are not certain that this is the explanation for three men appearing, we can be certain that it was the Lord who was present. It is exciting to read the words "Is anything too hard for the Lord?" That does mean that impossible is not a word in God's vocabulary! It is also interesting to note that the Lord did confront Sarah when she denied she had laughed, saying, "No, but you did laugh." No falsehood is allowed in the presence of the one who is the truth!

DAY 5

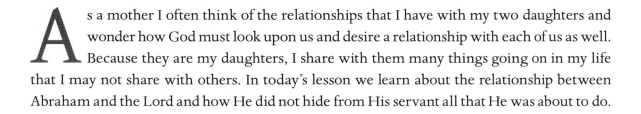

And the LORD said, "Shall I hide from Abraham what I am doing, since Abraham shall surely become a great and mighty nation, and all the nations of the earth shall be blessed in him?"
—Genesis 18:17

Prayer First: _____

_____

As a mother I often think of the relationships that I have with my two daughters and wonder how God must look upon us and desire a relationship with each of us as well. Because they are my daughters, I share with them many things going on in my life that I may not share with others. In today's lesson we learn about the relationship between Abraham and the Lord and how He did not hide from His servant all that He was about to do.

Let's pick up in Genesis 18:16–33.

From verses 16–19 what do we learn about the relationship between Abraham and the Lord and why the Lord wanted that relationship?

It is very worthwhile to step back and give thought to Abraham's relationship with God and what we can learn from this passage about why God wanted a relationship with him. The phrase "Shall I hide from Abraham what I am doing?" is remarkable. For God to make this statement and then to reveal to Abraham His future plan for Sodom and Gomorrah surely indicates that there existed a close walk between Abraham and his God. But what I find even more exciting is what God states are His clear purposes for knowing Abraham! Let's take a close look at those purposes in verse 19 and consider how they could apply in our lives as well.

1. "In order that he may command his children and his household after him, that they keep the way of the Lord."

   For Abraham to be able to pass on to his children and grandchildren the understanding of the way of God, he himself had to have an understanding of the way of the Lord. We too must have that knowledge and perception of the things of God which have been revealed to us by His Holy Spirit. By teaching our children God's way and allowing them to witness in our lives the very presence of the Lord Jesus Christ, we can enable God's purpose of keeping His way to be fulfilled in their lives.

2. "To do righteousness and justice."

   This phrase is stating exactly what Abraham's offspring must do in order to keep the way of the Lord. They were to do what was right and they were to do what was just. God's righteousness and justice will always be evident in a life that chooses these things.

3. "That the Lord may bring to Abraham what He has spoken to him."

    God reaffirms in verse 18 His call and purpose upon Abraham's life: that he "shall surely become a great and mighty nation, and all the nations of the earth shall be blessed in him." For this to be fulfilled, God was setting apart a people to become His own. God would complete in Abraham what He had promised, but for that to happen, the descendants of Abraham must know the way of the Lord by walking righteously and justly before Him.

We may think that God's purpose and plan for Abraham's life was far greater than His plan for ours. What we must remember is that it is not really about Abraham, and it is not really about us. It is all about God. When our focus begins to shift away from ourselves, then our God will begin to say of us, "Shall I hide from my servant what I am about to do?"

    The Lord shares with Abraham that the outcry against Sodom and Gomorrah is great. Who or where might this clamor be coming from?

    Do you believe that presently there is an outcry to God concerning our nation, the United States?

From verses 23–33 list now what is spoken by Abraham to the Lord. Then list the Lord's response.

Abraham's words   The Lord's response

What can we learn from Abraham's example concerning interceding in prayer for others and interceding in prayer for cities and nations?

As we examine this passage in Genesis 18 we learn that an outcry against the perversion and grave sins of Sodom and Gomorrah rises to the very hearing of a holy and righteous God. Justice surely is soon to come. One might wonder if Abraham's continual requests on behalf of the righteous in Sodom might have crossed a line with the Lord. It certainly seemed that Abraham was very fearful of making the Lord angry by his persistent questioning. But surely the patience and justice of God were evident, because even in the event that only ten righteous could be found in the land, the Lord declared he would not destroy the land for the sake of the ten.

One definition of the word *attribute* includes "characteristic or quality of a certain person." From your study thus far, what attributes of the Lord do you find displayed in the story of the life of Abraham.

Looking back on this chapter and our entire study, I am amazed at the marvelous exhibition of the attributes of God throughout. As we discover these qualities of God and their uniqueness to His character, we can marvel as we ourselves come to know Him in new ways. This brings about the inevitable truth that the more we know God, the more we want to know God!

WEEK 4

Sodom and Gomorrah to Promises Fulfilled

But Isaac spoke to Abraham his father and said, "My father!"
And he said, "Here I am, my son."
Then he said, "Look, the fire and the wood, but where is the lamb for a burnt offering?"
And Abraham said, "My son, God will provide for Himself the lamb
for a burnt offering." So the two of them went together.
—Genesis 22:7–8

DAY 1

❧

For the wrath of God is revealed from heaven against all ungodliness and
unrighteousness of men, who suppress the truth in unrighteousness, because what
may be known of God is manifest in them, for God has shown it to them.
—Romans 1:18–19

Prayer First: _____

_____

❧

Isn't it exciting to experience God's Word in such a way that it could be described as an unending fountain of flowing waters of truth? But truth is not just a word; it is a person, the Lord Jesus Christ! How fascinating that in the Old Testament many years before the birth of Christ, God is setting in motion the plan for His arrival upon the earth!

The story of Sodom continues in chapter 19 as God reveals the depravity that has overtaken this city and the city of Gomorrah as well. But as we move ahead in our final week of study, brace yourself not only for what Lot and his family experience in Sodom but also for the revelation of promises fulfilled!

Read Genesis 19; Ruth 4:1–2.

When the two angels entered Sodom they found Lot sitting at the city gates. From reading the Ruth passage and your understanding about the cities in this culture, what might sitting at the city gates indicate?

If Lot was in a leadership position in the city of Sodom, surely he was aware of the abominable acts that were rampant in the city. Does this in anyway compare to leaders in our government and how easily they can get ensnared in the life of their cities, nation, etc.?

Read 2 Kings 6:8–18. What do you find in this passage that is similar to the story of Lot and the two angels we read about in Genesis 19:1–11?

We discover that God allowed those who were depraved to the point of moral blindness to also become physically blind. The confusion that followed in both accounts surely was God's way of sparing the lives of His people. One notable point is the interesting contrast that we find concerning Elisha's servant in the 2 Kings passage. Because of the prayer of Elisha this man was granted miraculous sight which in turn was God's way of calming his fears by revealing to him the protection that surrounded him. The severity of the perversion and immorality in Sodom is revealed to us through this story of Lot and the two angels. One could hardly be surprised at the wrath of God that is soon to come.

Read Romans 1:18–32; Luke 17:26–37.

From these passages and Genesis 19, list all that you learn about the wrath of God.

For example, Luke 17:37 says, "Wherever the body is, there the eagles will be gathered together."

> Where the body lies the vultures will gather.
> Where the sin lies judgment will occur.

The two men sent by God to destroy the cities warned Lot to remove his family, saying, "Take them out of this place!" As much as you can gather from the Genesis 19 passage, describe how Lot and each one of his family members responded to this warning.

Lot

Lot's wife

Lot's sons-in-law

Lots daughters

What does this Scripture seem to indicate about who is responsible for the protection of families?

Do you believe that today's society in the United States reflects that husbands and fathers take seriously their role as protector of their families? Why or why not?

Taking a look at the responses to the warnings that were given to Lot's family members can shed light upon the situation in a way that we today might relate to. The patriarch Lot appeared to be the only one who took these warnings seriously. Many might claim his fault for being in the land of Sodom to begin with. But at this point he took heed to the instructions commanded by the men to remove his family from Sodom by going to his sons-in-law with warnings to leave the land. They did not, however, take seriously Lot's admonitions and advice; in fact, the passage states that they seemed to think he was joking. Could it have been because of what had appeared to be reservation on Lot's part because of his lingering and failing to depart quickly?

We see no mention of a warning given to Lot's daughters or a response from them if one was given. Could this indicate that God does clearly hold husbands and fathers responsible for the protection and well-being of their families? While we see much of this lacking in our society today, it is good to commend the many men who do take seriously their role as protectors of their families.

Finally we must not forget Lot's wife, whose story has been told and retold for hundreds of years. Was outright disobedience to her husband and to the Lord what led to her demise? Or was looking back at the city a result of not trusting God and refusing to leave without reservation? Possibly both. Whatever the reason was that she looked back, she had been warned not to. The very possibility that her life could be spared was because of God's mercy upon Lot.

Many lessons can be learned by us today from this story of Lot and his family. Listening to God and taking heed to His warnings surely should be at the top of that list!

From verse 29 what do we learn is the reason God spared Lot and his daughters form destruction in Sodom?

Obviously the wrath of God came upon Sodom and Gomorrah because the outcry against them was great before the Lord. According to Revelation 5:8, what else goes up to the Lord?

Considering that God spared Lot's life because of Abraham's prayers and that the bowls of incense in the Book of Revelation represented the prayers of saints, what can we learn about the importance of intercessory prayer for others?

While God is merciful and gracious the very nature of His character does not continue to tolerate sin. Because God is just, judgment will come as a result of sin. We learn in Romans 1 that God has placed within us an awareness of Himself so that people are without excuse. A society that continues to shake their fist in the face of God will not escape the wrath that is revealed from heaven against ungodliness. How grateful we should be that God hears our prayers when we intercede for others and for our nation. Let us take seriously the warnings of God we receive and plead to God for the salvation of our loved ones and of our nation.

Looking back on previous decisions made by Lot, are you surprised at what is occurring in his life in Genesis 19:30–38?

Since our study is on the life of Abraham we will not spend a lot of time discussing the story of the descendants of Lot shown to us in the latter part of Genesis 19. Still, it is worth noting that what appeared to be the right decision earlier in his life to choose the land of Sodom has certainly proved otherwise. Many lessons can be learned from observing the life of Lot. One huge one is that the decisions and choices we make affect not only our lives but the lives of those around us and even those in generations to come.

DAY 2

Then Abimelech took sheep, oxen, and male and female servants, and
gave them to Abraham; and he restored Sarah his wife to him.
—GENESIS 20:14

Prayer First: _____

_____

Have you ever found in your life that you have made a wrong choice, and it was not the first time that you had made that choice? I know I have, and at the time I clearly called upon the mercy of God to not allow in my life what I deserved for my actions. Maybe my thoughts were that God's mercy only extended for the first time and there were no more chances. While consequences will come for our actions and even sometimes God's discipline, God is merciful and gracious to us. In today's lesson we will learn of that same mercy and grace shown to Abraham and Sarah.

Read Genesis 20.

What details in this story of Abraham and Abimelech do you find that are similar to another time in the lives of Abraham and Sarah?

In seems that the Lord went to great lengths to keep Sarah from any physical contact with Abimelech. List possible reasons that the Lord did that.

This story seems to be repeating itself. Surely we remember back in chapter 12 the time that Abraham and Sarah spent in Egypt. Out of fear Abraham instructed his wife then, and now again in chapter 20, to state that she was Abraham's sister. Sarah was Abraham's half-sister, the daughter of his father but not his mother. But Sarah was Abraham's wife. This information was withheld in both instances. And on both occasions God's intervention protected Sarah from any physical relations she might have had with either man. Remember that Sarah had a divine purpose to fulfill. One might wonder if keeping her pure was to fulfill the purpose that she was to bear "the Son of the Promise."

DAY 3

*For Sarah conceived and bore Abraham a son in his old age, at
the set time of which God had spoken to him.*
—GENESIS 21:2

Prayer First: _____

_____

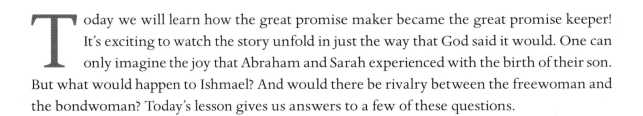

Today we will learn how the great promise maker became the great promise keeper!
It's exciting to watch the story unfold in just the way that God said it would. One can
only imagine the joy that Abraham and Sarah experienced with the birth of their son.
But what would happen to Ishmael? And would there be rivalry between the freewoman and
the bondwoman? Today's lesson gives us answers to a few of these questions.

Read Genesis 21:1–21.

The promise had been fulfilled! Isaac was born to this elderly couple just as
God had declared would happen! List the details about all the happenings of
Isaac's birth, the promise fulfilled.

As we read of God's faithfulness to Sarah, we can be reminded of His faithfulness in our lives as well. Read verse 1 again. In place of the name Sarah put your name instead. Name ways that God visits you (as He has said). Also list what He does for you (that He has said He would do).

As you study about Hagar and Ishmael departing, what important principle (literally and spiritually) can you learn about the son of the bondwoman and the son of the freewoman remaining together?

Isn't it exciting to finally meet the son of the freewoman? Isaac was born to Abraham and Sarah just as God had promised. The Hebrew word for the name Isaac is *Yitschaq*, pronounced "yits-khawk," meaning "laughter." At one time Sarah laughed at the idea of her bearing a child in her old age. Now the laugh is surely on her! From Isaac would come the nation of Israel—a nation that God chose to set apart for Himself, a nation that was a part of God's providential plan for the redemption of mankind, and a nation from which, many generations later, came the Chosen One, the Lord Jesus Christ!

In the second section of chapter 21 we learn about the departure of Hagar and Ishmael. While it was heartbreaking to Abraham, God clearly affirmed to Abraham that this was His will. God demonstrated his goodness and kindness to Hagar and Ishmael when He provided for them in the wilderness and also revealed to Hagar the future that was in store for her son. While God showed His physical provision for Hagar and Ishmael, a spiritual principle we can take from this passage is that God does not intend for the "son of the bondwoman" to remain with the "son of the freewoman." One has to be cast out! In your life which one will it be?

Read Genesis 21:22–34.

From this passage list the reasons for a covenant between Abraham and Abimelech, and also list details we learn of this covenant.

Can you think of any important ways this covenant differed from "the Abrahamic covenant" that God made with Abraham?

Compared to our earlier studies of covenants, this particular one is first of its kind mentioned in the Bible. This binding agreement was made between two equal parties. The previous two that we studied were covenants that God initiated between Himself and humans. It appears that Abimelech was very much aware of God's hand upon the life of Abraham. It is not certain whether Abimelech wanted an agreement with Abraham because of fear of Abraham's God or because he hoped to receive some of that favor as well.

It is interesting to note that while Abimelech was not aware that an issue existed between the two, Abraham did confront this issue before proceeding with the covenant. It is also noteworthy to mention that after the making of the covenant, Abraham planted a tamarisk tree which could be called a grove. He also called on the name of the Lord, the everlasting God. While it seems that throughout his life Abraham sometimes got out of the will of God, it is very evident that in most of the happenings of his life reverence and acknowledgement of God always occurred.

DAY 4

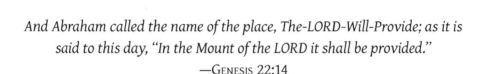

*And Abraham called the name of the place, The-LORD-Will-Provide; as it is
said to this day, "In the Mount of the LORD it shall be provided."*
—Genesis 22:14

Prayer First: _____

_____

O ur study today includes the story of one of the most telling examples of faith in God
told throughout the Scriptures. This particular passage may be very difficult for some
to study and understand. It demonstrates that while God had a destination planned
for Abraham, that destination clearly would be reached by faith. This test was most certainly
the test of all tests.

Read Genesis 22:1–19.

What do you learn in verse 1 about why God is telling Abraham to sacrifice
his son, Isaac?

Can you think of and share a time in your life when God has allowed you to go through a very difficult test?

What can we learn about Abraham from the statement he made in verse 5 about who would be returning with him to the young men?

We have learned that we cannot know the thoughts of God, but one might wonder just what the Lord was thinking as He looked upon Abraham and saw such a great measure of faith. What we can know for sure is what Scripture states about faith and trusting in God.

Record here what you have learned from God's Word of these very truths revealed. Share any passages of Scripture that you might have committed to memory in regard to faith and trust in God as they apply in the context of this story. (Remember all you have learned about being justified by faith.)

Just as Abraham was about to sacrifice Isaac, what did God provide?

Read Matthew 27:15–26; Luke 23:13–25.

As we near the end of our study on the life of Abraham, consider the story of Barabbas. What picture could Barabbas's story foreshadow, and how can it be compared to Isaac's story and your story?

The agony of a father ascending a mountain in order to sacrifice his "begotten son" is beyond description. Could this be compared to how our heavenly Father must have agonized over the sacrifice of His "Only Begotten"?

Isaac was willing to do his father's will, just as the Lord Jesus surrendered to the will of His Heavenly Father. The scene changes as Isaac becomes a type of lost and sinful people condemned to die. A substitute was provided for Isaac, just as the Lord Jesus became a substitute for Barabbas and on the cross for all mankind. What a glorious picture of redemption God reveals in these passages. When Abraham passed the test by fearing God and did not even withhold his own son from Him, God did not require Abraham to slay him. He Himself was the only one who experienced that pain and suffering when His only-begotten Son was sacrificed.

Read Genesis 22:20 through Genesis 24:9; Genesis 25:1–11.

From reading these remaining chapters of the life of Abraham, what do we learn about how his final years were spent and what responsibilities he took during his old age?

How good and gracious is our God as He has revealed to us in Genesis 11–25 so many details of this one man's life. In the final chapters He even allows us to recognize that Abraham finished strong in the race of life. We can learn from Abraham's example that in each endeavor of life we must complete and fulfill the purpose to which God has called us. Oh but thanks be to God that He Himself will complete that purpose through us!

> *Being confident of this, that*
> *he who began a good work in you*
> *will carry it on to completion*
> *until the day of Christ Jesus.*
> —Philippians 1:6 NIV

DAY 5

"Behold, the days are coming, says the LORD, when I will make a new covenant with the house of Israel and with the house of Judah
—JEREMIAH 31:31

Prayer First: _____

_____

After prayer and much consideration I have decided it would be amiss not to include one more covenant that I believe will make this story complete. As our study nears the end and we find the purpose of Abraham's life being fulfilled, I am grateful that while God made a covenant with Abraham thousands of years ago, we are the beneficiaries of the new covenant God made through our Lord Jesus Christ.

Read Jeremiah 31:31–34; Mark 14:22–26; Luke 22:14–22; Hebrews 8:6–13; 9:15; 12:24.

As you consider these passages on the new covenant, record here all the details you learn of this more "excellent" covenant.

Reflect back now on our study and particularly God's call on Abraham's life in Genesis 12.

How could the new covenant you have just read about be relevant in any way to God's promise to Abraham that "in you all families on earth shall be blessed"?

From Jeremiah's prophetic mention of this new and more excellent covenant to the actual institution of it recorded in the Gospels, one could certainly state that just two questions hardly do justice to this amazing act of God. Most assuredly a whole Bible study itself could be written on this very subject.

> *And for this reason He is the Mediator of the new covenant, by means of death, for the redemption of the transgressions under the first covenant, that those who are called may receive the promise of the eternal inheritance.*
> —HEBREWS 9:15

At this point in our study you have learned about the Abrahamic covenant, the old covenant (the Law), and now the new covenant. God promised Abraham in the Abrahamic covenant that he would become a great nation, and from that nation would come the One through whom all families on earth would be blessed. While Israel under the Mosaic old covenant was physical fulfillment of the Abrahamic covenant's promise, the new covenant is the spiritual fulfillment of that promise. No longer would God's law be written on stone but now would be written on human hearts.

Interesting to consider is the fact that in the Old Testament God initiated these covenants, and in the New Testament Jesus Himself initiated the new covenant. This is just a clear reminder of God's goodness shown to us as He has continually reached out to us in grace.

Surely our God is a covenant-making and covenant-keeping God!

For the last question of our study, reflect on God's faithfulness shown to Abraham throughout his life. Record here the many ways that you have recognized that faithfulness shown.

After recording these ways in Abraham's life, look back upon your own life, and record His faithful ways demonstrated in your life as well.

As we complete our study on the life of Abraham, may we be reminded of the complete faithfulness that was shown by God to His servant Abraham. Beginning with the moment that God called him in Genesis 12, we recognize God's faithful hand upon his life in a profound way. Even when Abraham and Sarah wavered and ended up in Egypt, God protected them and did not allow them to stay there. His sovereign hand was upon them as He brought them back to the land He had promised to them, the land of Canaan. God was faithful as He used Abraham and his allies to rescue Lot in the Valley of Siddim and also blessed him through Melchizedek, King of Salem and Priest of God Most High. His faithfulness was displayed as He gave the Abrahamic covenant, His promise to Abraham and his descendants and ultimately that promise to be fulfilled through Abraham's seed, Lord Jesus Christ.

God was faithful in that even again when Sarah and Abraham took matters into their own hands by bringing Hagar and Ishmael into their lives, this did not thwart the plan that God had for them, the plan that would come through their offspring Isaac, "the promised son." A faithful God gave to Abraham the sign of the covenant through circumcision and also, when changing their names, declared to Abraham that he would become the father of many and Sarah would become the mother of nations. God was faithful when coming to Abraham and Sarah to announce that in the next year Isaac would be born.

His faithfulness was shown by confiding in Abraham about the wrath that was to come upon Sodom, his nephew Lot's dwelling place. God was faithful in that He remembered His servant Abraham and rescued Lot and his daughters from Sodom before destroying Sodom and Gomorrah. Faithfulness and patience again were shown to Abraham when Sarah ended up in King Abimelech's household just as she had ended up earlier in Pharaoh's household in Egypt. God protected Sarah by keeping her pure and allowing no physical contact between her and these kings. He also protected Abraham's life in both these settings. Not only did He protect Abraham, but later He allowed Abraham to enter into a covenant with Abimelech which allowed for peaceful dwelling with those around him.

Now the big event occurred! Isaac, the promised son, was born! God had been faithful. God knew that after that the son of the bondwoman could not remain with the son of the freewoman. One had to be cast out. In his compassion and faithfulness God provided for Hagar and her son.

Surely the greatest indicator of all of the faithfulness of God was when He allowed Abraham to be tested. But instead of requiring the life of Abraham's begotten son Isaac, God provided a substitute. What a picture of God's faithfulness to you and me! Instead of requiring our lives as the sacrifice for our sins, God provided that sacrifice Himself—in fact providing Himself through Abraham's seed, the man our Lord Jesus Christ!

When looking back and recognizing the faithfulness of God in Abraham's life, I begin to think about His faithfulness in my life as well. While Abraham's story is unique, each one of our lives is unique to God as well. As God was faithful to Abraham, so He will be to you and me!

God used Abraham in a mighty way as a part of the redemption plan that He had for humankind. As Abraham walked on this journey, one might ask whether he understood the significant role he played in this plan. Could he possibly have known that thousands of years later you and I, like many others, would read his story and hang on its every word?

Abraham had many encounters with God. I believe that a flame of fire is lit in a life that has had an encounter with God. The flame burns within that individual in such a way that nothing else compares. No other relationship or cause for living, as important as they may be, keeps that flame burning. Only the eternal God of the universe who lights the flame fuels the fire—a fire that burns for all eternity!